Aluminum Foil

REMOVE RUST SPOTS

and Other Household Hints

Betsy Rossen Elliot

Contents

Maintenance and Projects • 2

Housecleaning and Housekeeping • 9

Cooking, Baking & Washing Up • 14

Feeling Good, Looking Good • 19

Arts & Crafts, Pets & Pastimes • 23

Maintenance and Projects

Whether you're known as Car Guy, Handy Annie, The Gardener, or *Tool Time* cast member, the kitchen pantry has some tips just for you. Check out the qualified help you'll find in aluminum foil, wax paper, other wraps and clings, and more. And, of course, there's always duct tape!

CAR CARE

◆ To get rid of rust spots on chrome bumpers, scrub with Pepsi; use a wadded-up piece of Reynolds Wrap Aluminum Foil as a scrubber.

◆ You can also clean battery terminals with the above method. Dip a piece of Reynolds Wrap Aluminum Foil in Pepsi and use it to scrub.

◆ Need a pan to catch oil drips while working on the car? Flatten a cardboard box, cover it with Reynolds Wrap Aluminum Foil, and tape it down with Scotch Duct Tape.

◆ Make a sun reflector for your car's windshield by cutting a piece of cardboard to fit, covering the cardboard with Reynolds Wrap Aluminum Foil, and taping down the foil with Scotch Duct Tape.

◆ Scotch Duct Tape can do effective—though not aesthetically pleasing—emergency auto work, such as reattaching a windshield wiper arm, reconnecting a tailpipe, or patching a taillight cover.

- If you don't have a garage and a snowstorm is coming, cover your car's side mirrors with a GLAD Food Storage Zipper Bag held in place by clothespins or rubber bands. You won't have to scrape them later.

PAINTING TIME

- Use Reynolds Wrap Heavy Strength Aluminum Foil or Reynolds Wrap Super Strength Aluminum Foil to protect exterior hardware, including doorknobs, window frames, and awning brackets, from paint. The foil adapts to a variety of shapes and comes off easily when you're done painting.

- When painting with a roller, save cleanup time by lining your paint tray with Reynolds Wrap Aluminum Foil before adding the paint. When you're through, simply throw the foil away.

- If you're not done with a painting job, wrap your paintbrushes with Reynolds Wrap Aluminum Foil and put them in the refrigerator or freezer until you're ready to go back to work.

- Reynolds Wrap Aluminum Foil can prevent a "crust" from forming on leftover paint. Place the paint can on a piece of foil and trace around the bottom of it. Cut out the foil circle, lay it gently atop the paint's surface, and seal the can.

- Instead of sponge-painting walls or furniture, ball up a piece of Reynolds Cut-Rite Wax Paper. Dip it in the paint and dab away for a new effect.

- For small cracks in plaster, make your own patching compound with Elmer's Glue-All and ARM & HAMMER Baking Soda. Mix enough glue with the baking soda to make a paste, then fill cracks and let dry before painting.

- To paint a straight line, stretch a rubber band around the middle of the bristles on your paintbrush to keep them tight (but not bunched up). Dip the brush into the paint up to the rubber band.

HOW DOES YOUR GARDEN GROW?

Green House Tips

- Help household plants that need a lot of sunlight: Line a windowsill with Reynolds Wrap Aluminum Foil to increase the sun's reflection. This is great for cacti and geraniums.

- To keep cuttings upright in a jar of water, stretch a piece of Reynolds Wrap Aluminum Foil over the jar and poke holes in the foil using a toothpick. Insert the stems through the holes.

- If you keep your seedlings on a windowsill before bringing them outside, surround them on 3 sides with a folded piece of cardboard covered with Reynolds Wrap Aluminum Foil to bring in as much light as possible.

- Transform cores from rolls of Reynolds Wrap Aluminum Foil and Scott Towels into mini seed-starting pots. Cut the cardboard tubes into pieces about 3 inches long. Wrap the outside (but not the ends) of each with aluminum foil to keep the cardboard from falling apart when wet. Put the "pots," closely packed, in a waterproof tray or shallow pan. Fill each with seed-starting mix and plant the seeds. When they're ready, remove the foil and plant the seedlings, pots and all.

- Here's another seed incubator idea: Line a shoebox with Reynolds Wrap Aluminum Foil, shiny side up; allow the foil to extend over the sides about 2 inches. Punch several draining holes in the bottom of the box, through the foil, and fill the box slightly more than half-way with potting soil. Plant the seeds, place box near a sunny window, and keep the soil moist. The foil will reflect light and absorb heat for the seedlings.

- Yet another seed-starter substitute is an ice cube tray. Punch drainage holes in the bottom; set tray in a shallow pan, then follow directions in above tip.

Four Syllables or Five?

English chemist Sir Humphry Davy discovered and named a new element in 1807. He first spelled it *alumium,* then changed it to *aluminum,* and finally settled on *aluminium* in 1812. In the 1890s, the metal became widely available and a subject in print; in the United States, Noah Webster's 1828 dictionary used only *aluminum,* but it took the better part of 75 years for that to catch on as the popular choice. The American Chemical Society officially adopted *-um* in 1925. When the International Union of Pure and Applied Chemistry decided to standardize the spelling as *-ium* in 1990, the population for the most part overlooked it, continuing to spell it *-um.* And that's still how it's listed by Webster's today.

◆ Slow down the evaporation of moisture from a house-plant when you go out of town. After watering, wrap the pot and soil in GLAD Cling Wrap. Have it touch the stem, folded loosely over the soil.

Your Own Acreage

◆ If your crop of cucumbers or squash seems threatened by munching bugs, cut up small strips of Reynolds Wrap Aluminum Foil and use them as mulch. The shiny substance scares away some light-sensitive pests.

◆ If deer are nibbling at the bark of a young tree, protect it by wrapping the trunk with Reynolds Wrap Aluminum Foil. The foil should be at least as high as your waist. This method can also deter mice and rabbits.

◆ If insects are climbing the trunk of your fruit tree, wrap it with strips of Reynolds Wrap Aluminum Foil. The bugs can't get traction on the slick foil.

◆ Shoo birds away from fruit trees by using fishing line to hang lots of twisted strips of Reynolds Wrap Aluminum Foil. The reflected light and sound will do the job.

◆ Pouring a garden solution from bucket to bottle is no "neat trick"... unless you make a garden funnel. Place a sheet of Reynolds Cut-Rite Wax Paper on a sheet of newspaper. Roll it up into a cone, with the wax paper inside. Insert the tip of the cone in the bottle; pour.

◆ Sore knees after a long day of gardening? Make kneeling pads by cutting 3 or 4 layers of Reynolds Cut-Rite Wax Paper into squares to place on the ground. If you're working in a small garden patch or bed, put down a triple-layer strip of wax paper to cover the entire length of the bed.

◆ Rose thorns and cactus needles can pierce even thick work gloves. Before you put them on, wrap small strips of Scotch Duct Tape around your fingers and thumbs.

MAINTENANCE DEPARTMENT

◆ Missing irregularly shaped pieces of flagstone on a walkway? Place a piece of Reynolds Wrap Aluminum Foil over the spot, then press down the edges to make a template of the needed shape. With a nail, trace around the template to transfer the pattern onto flagstone; cut stone to pattern.

◆ To reflect the heat of the summer sun, staple or tape sheets of Reynolds Wrap Aluminum Foil to the inside of your roof, between the studs. The heat entering your house can be reduced by at least 20 percent.

◆ Make a messy job much easier: Instead of dealing with encrusted soot on the bottom of a charcoal grill or a fireplace, first line it with Reynolds Wrap Heavy Strength Aluminum Foil. When the fire is out and the foil is completely cooled, ball it up and toss it in the trash.

◆ Boost the efficiency of your heating: To deflect heat into a room instead of into the wall behind it, wrap a piece of cardboard or wood with Reynolds Wrap Heavy Strength Aluminum Foil, shiny side out. Place it below a baseboard vent, behind a floor register, or behind a radiator unit, angling it however it best deflects heat toward the center of the room.

- To block drafts coming from a warped storm window, raise the lower sash of the window and apply a ribbon of caulk on the sill. Place a piece of GLAD Cling Wrap over the caulk, then lower the sash and lock it. Raise it when the caulk dries; remove the plastic wrap. Custom-fitted weather stripping!

- Who needs a vise when you've got duct tape? Attach the items to be joined to a workbench or other surface with Scotch Duct Tape.

- O-Cel-O sponges, attached to work pants with Scotch Duct Tape, become comfy knee pads for any handy-person, painter, or gardener.

- Need to saw in a really tight space? Wrap one end of a hacksaw blade with Scotch Duct Tape to make a handle. (This is also a great tool for freeing windows that have been painted shut.)

- Those leaves and other yard debris caught between the boards of a deck hold moisture and can lead to decay. Attach a putty knife or a screwdriver to a broom or mop handle with Scotch Duct Tape. Use the new tool to push the debris down through the cracks.

- A drop of Instant Krazy Glue can repair a small hole in a screen.

Their Mothers Must Be So Proud

Jim Berg and Tim Nyberg have quite an attachment to duct tape. In fact, they are known as *the* authorities on everything duct tape and reveal their knowledge at ducttapeguys.com. Their books include *The Jumbo Duct Tape Book* and *Duct Shui*.

Housecleaning and Housekeeping

Aluminum foil and the other great products that are packaged on rolls are no strangers to household chores. They double their efforts and minimize your work. They keep the chaos under wraps. These household helpers can clean the kitchen like pros, help with appliance repair, and tend to the floors. Even Post-it Notes get in on the fun... and not just for reminders of what you need to do today!

KITCHEN PATROL

◆ Place a sheet of Reynolds Wrap Aluminum Foil on the floor of your freezer to keep spills and ice cube trays from sticking. Be sure not to cover any vents or other openings.

◆ If a lightly used Brillo Steel Wool Soap Pad still has some oomph left, don't throw it away. Wrap it in Reynolds Wrap Aluminum Foil (so it won't rust) and put it in the freezer.

◆ To remove silver tarnish, bring a medium-size pot of water to a boil and add ½ teaspoon Morton Salt and 1 to 2 teaspoons of ARM & HAMMER Baking Soda. Reduce heat. Place tarnished silverware and a piece of Reynolds Wrap Aluminum Foil in the pot. Simmer for 2 to 3 minutes. Rinse the silverware well, then use a soft cloth to buff dry.

- Keep silverware shiny by storing it on a sheet of Reynolds Wrap Aluminum Foil. To store it for the long term, first wrap each piece in GLAD Cling Wrap (squeeze out as much air as you can). Then wrap in foil, sealing the ends.

- Rub a piece of Reynolds Cut-Rite Wax Paper over your tile or laminate kitchen countertops. The shine will send you reaching for your sunglasses.

- Clip coupons and then forget them? Hold them together with a binder clip. Hang it on a magnetic refrigerator hook, on the bulletin board—anywhere you'll see the coupons and grab them on your way to the grocery store.

YOUR FLOOR AND MORE

- Reduce the strain of moving furniture over a smooth floor, such as tile or hardwood: Place pieces of Reynolds Wrap Aluminum Foil under the legs, shiny side up. The dull side is actually more slippery!

- Add extra shine to your clean, dry tile floor. Wrap a piece of Reynolds Cut-Rite Wax Paper around a dust mop and sweep it over the floor.

- Cover stains or burns in your carpet with a matching Crayola Crayon. Rub it into the spot, cover with Reynolds Cut-Rite Wax Paper, and lightly iron on low heat.

YOU CAN FIX THAT

◆ A broken spring in a battery-operated device can ruin it—unless you fold a small piece of Reynolds Wrap Aluminum Foil and use it to fill the gap.

◆ If the silver backing of a mirror wears off, tape a piece of Reynolds Wrap Aluminum Foil to the back with the shiny side toward the mirror.

◆ If the glue on a floor tile has dried out and the tile is coming up, you may be able to revive it. Cover the tile with a sheet of Reynolds Wrap Aluminum Foil and heat with an iron until the glue melts. Place a heavy object on the tile until the glue dries again.

◆ Repair damaged books with Scotch Duct Tape along the edges and spine.

◆ To fix a screw hole that has become too large to hold its screw, make a plug out of a Rite Aid cotton ball by soaking it in Elmer's Glue-All and stuffing it into the hole. Let dry, then reinsert the screw.

◆ You can also repair an enlarged screw hole by making a paste of sawdust and Elmer's Glue-All. Fill the hole, let the glue dry overnight, then reinsert the screw.

◆ Fill cracks and small gaps in wood, metal, and plastic by sprinkling ARM & HAMMER Baking Soda into the opening and then dripping Instant Krazy Glue over it until the gap is filled.

- Silence a squeaky floorboard by dribbling Elmer's Glue-All into the crack. Let dry overnight before walking on the floor again.

- If the heating element of a space heater touches the reflector behind it, it's a dangerous situation. Make sure the appliance is unplugged, then use an unbent large paper clip to gently pull the element away from the reflector.

HANDY TO KNOW

- To lengthen the life of unused batteries, put them in a GLAD Food Storage Zipper Bag, and store in a cool, dry place.

- Electronic components stacked on top of each other—such as a TV and a DVD player—can result in electro-magnetic interference. Prevent the problem by placing a sheet of Reynolds Wrap Aluminum Foil between them.

- Before clamping just-glued wood furniture, wrap the joint with Reynolds Cut-Rite Wax Paper. It will protect the surface from marring.

- Prevent toddlers from locking themselves in the bath-room (or any room). Wrap the door handle in the unlocked position with a piece of GLAD Press'n Seal.

- Protect books by covering them with a sheet of GLAD Press'n Seal.

- Put a rubber band around each spray bottle and other product containers. Tuck an O-Cel-O sponge or clean cloth under the band so you'll always have one at hand.

- If a key breaks in a lock, put a touch of Instant Krazy Glue on the broken-off part. Insert that part into the lock, wait a few seconds, and pull out the rest of the key.

- To hang work gloves, caps, sun hats, or any bulky item on a pegboard, use an extra-large binder clip.

- Use an ice cube tray to keep small items organized on a workbench, counter, or other work surface.

- When a big carton proclaims, "Some Assembly Required," chances are it contains a bag of hardware. Use an ice cube tray to separate all those nuts, bolts, screws, washers, clips, and the like to make assembling easier.

MORE HOUSECLEANING AND HOUSEKEEPING TIPS

- The same chemical process that removes tarnish from silver—ion exchange—can be used to clean jewelry. Line a small bowl with Reynolds Wrap Aluminum Foil. Fill the bowl with hot water and stir in 1 tablespoon Tide powdered laundry detergent. Soak jewelry in the solution for 1 minute, then rinse well and let dry.

- Use a Post-it Note to clean a keyboard—whether piano or computer! Run the sticky side between the keys to pick up crumbs and lint.

Cooking, Baking & Washing Up

You can almost hear the wax paper, aluminum foil, plastic wraps, and their pals shouting, "Let us at that kitchen! We were born and rolled to be here!" What they have in store is way beyond covering the turkey and wrapping up leftovers. Foil, plastic wrap, and clips save you time and effort. What's more, somebody let the ice cube trays out of the freezer, and they have some cool new ideas for you.

PREP WORK

◆ Spread a sheet of Reynolds Wrap Aluminum Foil on the oven rack below a baking pan if you fear boilovers and spills. (Don't spread the foil on the bottom of an oven.)

◆ The brown sugar is hard as a rock! Don't run to the store for a fresh bag; simply chip off a chunk, wrap it in Reynolds Wrap Aluminum Foil, and bake it at 300°F for 5 minutes to soften.

◆ Before you prepare food on a countertop, cover the surface with a large sheet of either Reynolds Cut-Rite Wax Paper or Reynolds Parchment Paper. Put it under any cutting boards too. This is especially important when working with meat, chicken, or fish.

 ◆ Egg yolks can last 3 days in the fridge in a covered container. Press GLAD Cling Wrap directly on the surface of

broken yolks. Submerge unbroken ones in water to keep them moist.

- ◆ Cover a food scale with GLAD Press'n Seal for quicker measurements and cleanup.

- ◆ Bunch together produce such as fresh parsley, chives, and scallions with a rubber band for easier chopping.

BAKING BITS

- ◆ Want to make a special-shape cake but don't have the exact pan? Create that heart, teddy bear, football, or whatever-you-please by forming the shape with a double thickness of Reynolds Wrap Heavy Strength Aluminum Foil. Place the shape inside a large cake pan; pour in the batter.

- ◆ Decorate that cake with a "pastry bag" made of Reynolds Wrap Heavy Strength Aluminum Foil. Form the foil into a tube with a small opening at the tip, fill it with easily flowing frosting, and pipe your design.

- ◆ To bake a pie to golden brown without burning the edges of the crust, cover those edges with strips of Reynolds Wrap Aluminum Foil.

- ◆ Cake layers can be baked up to 2 days in advance, individually wrapped in GLAD Cling Wrap, and kept in the refrigerator.

Wrap Session

GLAD Cling Wrap won't stick to itself if stored in the refrigerator or freezer. To unsnarl a piece of GLAD Cling Wrap, have it chill out in the freezer for about 10 minutes.

- What's the secret to perfectly round homemade refrigerator cookies? Cut a vertical slit down the length of a Scott Towels cardboard core, then line the inside with GLAD Cling Wrap. Fill the tube with dough, evenly and completely, and overlap plastic wrap to close. Fit the tube edges back together; secure the shape with rubber bands or tape. Refrigerate until ready to bake.

MORE KITCHEN TIPS

- Shape a piece of Reynolds Wrap Aluminum Foil into a cone, and use it as a funnel.

- Did you know the handiest low-fat cheese spread is yogurt? Put plain, nonfat yogurt in a Melitta Cone Coffee Filter, stand filter in a tall container, cover the filter with GLAD Cling Wrap, and let it drain overnight in the refrigerator. Flavor the yogurt cheese with any herb of choice, and use it as a cracker or sandwich spread.

- Protect recipe cards and cookbook pages from splatters by covering them with GLAD Press'n Seal.

- If you know you'll be in and out of the refrigerator with messy hands, wrap a piece of GLAD Press'n Seal around the door handle before you start cooking.

- Use a large rubber band to deal with a stubborn jar lid. Wrap band around edge of lid, and give lid a good twist.

- Freeze leftover stock, broth, cooking wine, and other liquids in an ice cube tray. Measure and note the capacity of each compartment. You'll have ready-to-use recipe ingredients.

Just Two Words: Plastic Wrap

In 1933, a Dow Chemical lab worker accidentally discovered leftover goo: polyvinylidene chloride. The greasy, green, smelly film was dubbed "Saran" and was used by the military as a coating to protect World War II fighter planes from the elements. Dow eliminated the color and odor and introduced Saran Wrap plastic film for commercial use in 1949 and household use in 1953. The Saran brand was acquired by S. C. Johnson in 1998.

◆ Binder clips are a great help in the kitchen: Use them to attach recipes to the oven hood while cooking; close pourable cartons, condiment packages, and snack bags; and clip up long shirt sleeves.

ORDER'S UP!

◆ To create a special warming aid for serving bread, rolls, and baked goods straight from the oven, place a piece of Reynolds Wrap Aluminum Foil under a napkin in a serving basket. This not only keeps the heat in but also keeps grease stains off the basket.

◆ Keep the mess to a minimum! To keep ice cream cones and watermelon slices drip-free, wrap the bottoms with Reynolds Wrap Aluminum Foil.

◆ Use a generous sheet of GLAD Press'n Seal to cover a toddler's chair at mealtime. Stay close by to make sure the child does not begin to play with the sheet.

- Save space and keep place mats handy by hanging them inside a pantry or cabinet door. Clip a set together with a binder clip.

- Group cloth napkin sets together in a drawer or hall pantry with a binder clip. When it's time to set the table for company, you'll have a full set at the ready.

DOIN' THE DISHES

- Reynolds Wrap Aluminum Foil can help loosen food cooked onto cast-iron pots and pans. Ball up a piece of foil; use it to rub away the mess. Wipe pot or pan clean with a soft, dry cloth.

- Cleaning a barbecue grill usually ranks among the least-savored chores. Try this: Lay a sheet of Reynolds Wrap Aluminum Foil on the grill while it's still hot. When it's cool, peel off the foil, scrunch it into a ball, and use it to rub the grill clean.

- Secure stemware and other delicate items to the dishwasher rack with rubber bands.

- Running O-Cel-O sponges and scrubbers through the dishwasher now and then is a good idea. Attach them to a rack with a binder clip if you think they might fall and clog the drain.

Feeling Good, Looking Good

Your family's health and well-being are top priorities for you. So are saving time and money and reducing aggravation. The news is good, therefore, if you're open to grooming tips from a new kind of plastic wrap (GLAD Press'n Seal), beauty advice via Krazy Glue, and a home remedy straight off the roll of duct tape.

GROOMING AND REMEDIES

◆ Protect your specs from dye while your hair is being colored. Wrap the temples of your eyeglasses with small pieces of Reynolds Wrap Aluminum Foil. Now you can read while waiting.

◆ Line your makeup bag with GLAD Press'n Seal. Cleaning it out is a breeze. Press'n Seal is also an ideal solution for a broken case: Cover cosmetics such as powders and blushes to prevent spills.

◆ Create a pouch out of GLAD Press'n Seal to contain leftover soaps, toiletries, Q-tips cotton swabs, and more.

◆ Leg and arm braces with Velcro straps always seem to stick to pants and sleeves. Wrap them in GLAD Press'n Seal to prevent sticking or snags.

◆ To remove a pesky splinter, squeeze a drop of Elmer's Glue-All over the tip of the splinter, let dry, and peel off. The splinter will stick to the glue.

- Use Instant Krazy Glue to repair a split or torn fingernail in an emergency.

- Remove a wart with Scotch Duct Tape. Put a piece over the offender, leave it on for 6 days (replace if necessary), and then remove it. Soak the wart in water; dry, then gently rub spot with an emery board or a pumice stone. Leave tape off overnight. Repeat the routine. Treatment can take up to 2 months.

- Splint that injured finger by taping it to its next-door neighbor with Scotch Duct Tape. If you have any doubts about the severity of the injury, go to an emergency room.

- When you need to get your hair out of your eyes and you don't have a barrette on hand, use a small or medium-size binder clip to tuck those tresses out of the way.

- A large binder clip placed on the end of a tube of Crest toothpaste or similar packaging will assure that you'll get all your money's worth.

The Rollout

Duct tape was first created around 1942 by Johnson & Johnson. The military needed to keep moisture off ammunition cases; the remedy was tape made with cotton duck, similar to that used in cloth medical tapes. The waterproof wonder soon became known as "duck tape."

Duck tape was also used to fix World War II guns, vehicles, aircraft, canteens, and more. The postwar housing boom presented new taping opportunities, such as heating and air-conditioning connections. Its color was changed from army green to ductwork silver, and people referred to it as "duct tape." The name stuck.

- Freeze skin lotions and gels (such as aloe vera) in plastic ice cube trays. You'll get quick, cool relief for insect bites, rashes, chapped hands, sunburn, and other burns.

- Bring some order to that bathroom or bedroom drawer. A plastic ice cube tray is the perfect organizer for small items such as bobby pins, hair clips, safety pins, earrings, rings, and spare change.

THE IRONING OF IT ALL

- Cut your ironing time by putting a piece of Reynolds Wrap Aluminum Foil under the ironing board cover. The foil will reflect heat; you'll actually be ironing both sides at once.

- To remove built-up starch from an iron, pass it over a piece of Reynolds Wrap Aluminum Foil.

- Pleats will stay put with a large paper clip angled across them. From the wrong side of the fabric, iron from top to bottom. Be sure not to iron the clips.

CLOTHES-MOUTHED TIPS

- Make hangers glide over metal closet rods by first rubbing the rods with Reynolds Cut-Rite Wax Paper.

- You've spiffed up your shoes with Griffin Shoe Polish but don't want it to get on your clothes or furniture. When the polish has dried, wipe off any excess with a piece of Reynolds Cut-Rite Wax Paper.

- Garments falling off their hangers? Before you hang a garment, put a rubber band on each end of the hanger.

- Roll up thick magazines, secure with rubber bands, and place in tall boots to keep them upright.

FIXES AND FASTENERS

- Accidents happen, especially during potty training. In lieu of a plastic or rubber mattress pad, place several sheets of Reynolds Wrap Aluminum Foil across the width of a mattress. Cover them with a beach towel or two, then put on the mattress pad and bottom sheet.

- Those hard-to-fix bleach spots on clothes might be fixable with a Crayola Crayon. Pick a matching color, warm the fabric with an iron, and color the spot. Cover the spot with Reynolds Cut-Rite Wax Paper and iron on low to set the color.

- You can temporarily hold nonfusible interfacing in place with adhesive from an Elmer's Glue Stick. Instead of using pins and/or basting when making lapped seams, apply glue to the underside of the overlapping section. Press in place, let dry 1 or 2 minutes, and topstitch.

- Fix a falling hem in a pinch with a length of Scotch Duct Tape. It works especially well on heavy fabrics such as denim.

- Replace a missing zipper tab with a paper clip or a safety pin. Dress it up with a piece of ribbon or yarn or a dollop of paint.

Arts & Crafts, Pets & Pastimes

The art of enjoying life comes to us in many forms. Make the most of being creative, playing with the kids, petting a dog, picnicking with friends, cheering at a game, or taking a well-deserved vacation.

You'll have some help from some familiar convenience products. Press leaves in wax paper, learn golf from a binder clip, be more patient with your pet thanks to plastic wrap, and plan the perfect camping trip with aluminum foil. You deserve it!

FOR ARTISTS OF ALL AGES

- Make a disposable palette for paints by wrapping a piece of cardboard in Reynolds Wrap Aluminum Foil.

- If you need to stop a painting project midstream, instead of washing out your brush, tightly seal it in Reynolds Wrap Aluminum Foil or in a GLAD Food Storage Zipper Bag. The paint won't dry out before you return.

- Reynolds Parchment Paper is an excellent choice when you need tracing paper for any project.

- An ice cube tray makes a perfect paint palette, especially for very young artists.

- Line work surfaces with Reynolds Freezer Paper to prevent paint and glue stains.

FUN WITH THE KIDS

◆ Make a playing-card holder for young children with an empty box of Reynolds Wrap Aluminum Foil, Reynolds Cut-Rite Wax Paper, or GLAD Cling Wrap. Simply remove the cutting strip and close the lid. Stand the cards up between the flap and the side of the box. Paint or decorate the box with your child if desired.

◆ Make your own mosaic art with Post-it Notes.

Notes on Post-it Notes

1968: Spencer Silver, a 3M scientist, discovers a transferable adhesive.

1974: Another 3M employee, Art Fry, wants a semi-adhesive for use as a hymnal bookmark. Fry remembers his coworker's discovery, contacts Silver, and the two experiment with the adhesive on slips of paper. Fry is delighted with the results.

1977: Enough Post-it Notes are manufactured to supply 3M headquarters, and employees soon cannot do without them.

1978: 3M marketing floods the Idaho office supply industry with samples, and the reaction is amazing.

1979: Post-it Notes are introduced in 11 states. Office workers begin mailing the product to coworkers in the other 39 states.

1980: Post-it Notes are introduced nationwide. Everyone, from mail clerks to CEOs, loves Post-it Notes.

1981: Post-it Notes migrate to Canada and Europe.

2009: Post-it Notes are available in 62 colors, 25 shapes, and 8 standard sizes.

- To make a sun catcher, shave Crayola Crayons or colorful candle pieces onto a sheet of Reynolds Cut-Rite Wax Paper. Place another sheet on top, then put the whole set inside a paper grocery bag or between 2 sheets of cloth. Using a low setting, iron the "sandwich" until the shavings melt (try 10 seconds at first). Carefully remove the wax paper from the bag or cloth. Let the wax cool, then cut your sun catcher into a fun shape. Poke a hole near the top; use ribbon to hang it near a window.

- Here's a project from yester-year—creating place mats, bookmarks, book covers, or other decorative pieces. Arrange items such as colorful autumn  leaves, flowers, or magazine pictures on a sheet of Reynolds Cut-Rite Wax Paper. Cover with another sheet. Put the whole "sandwich" inside a paper grocery bag or between 2 sheets of cloth. Iron on low to melt the wax, creating a seal. Carefully remove the wax paper from the bag or cloth. Let it cool; cut it to the shape and size you wish. Use pinking shears to make interesting edges if you like.

- Most kids love stickers. But once they're stuck, they're stuck. Give kids a sheet of Reynolds Cut-Rite Wax Paper to put stickers on. They can arrange and rearrange the stickers to their hearts' content before putting them in a scrapbook or album.

- Cover your child's art project or photos with GLAD Press'n Seal to protect and preserve.

◆ A pack of Post-it Notes can lead to a pickup game of tic-tac-toe. Tailor the size of the notes to the playing surface as well as the child's age (bigger notes for younger kids).

◆ Here's a modeling clay recipe that's easy to make… and is no-bake! In a bowl, mix these ingredients in the following proportions: 1 part Elmer's Glue-All, 1 part Argo Corn Starch, 1 part Gold Medal All-Purpose Flour, and several drops of McCormick Food Color (optional). Turn out the mixture on a cutting board; knead it to the consistency of bread dough. Add more glue, corn starch, or flour if necessary. Make jewelry, ornaments, sculptures, or other creations. Air-dry; decorate with acrylic paint if desired. Store unused clay in a sealed container.

◆ Make your own colorful glues by using Elmer's Glue-All or Washable School Glue and adding a few drops of McCormick Food Color.

◆ Use Elmer's Glue-All and Reach dental floss to hang children's artwork. Apply glue to attach the floss to the back of the paper, or punch a small hole in the artwork and thread the floss through.

MORE CREATIVE TIPS

◆ Sharpen craft scissors by cutting a piece of Reynolds Wrap Aluminum Foil several times.

◆ Make ornaments or custom trays for serving holiday goodies. Cut decorative shapes out of cardboard, then cover the cardboard with Reynolds Wrap Aluminum Foil.

- Give a giant kiss! When the gift you bought presents a wrapping challenge, center it on a large round piece of cardboard (the cardboard from a frozen pizza would be a good choice). Tear a large sheet of Reynolds Wrap Heavy Strength Aluminum Foil from the roll, center the cardboard on top of the sheet, and fold the foil upward, twisting the ends together at the very top. Repeat, covering gift completely. To make a tag, cut a long, narrow strip of white paper and write the recipient's name on it. Attach it at the top of the "kiss."

- Use multicolored rubber bands in place of ribbon to decorate wrapped gifts.

- An empty box from Reynolds Wrap Aluminum Foil or another roll product—minus the cutting strip—is the perfect place to store knitting needles.

- To make a light-reflecting panel for photography, apply a light coat of rubber cement to heavy cardboard or mat board and cover with Reynolds Wrap Aluminum Foil, shiny side out. A handy approach is to make 3 panels and join them with silver Scotch Duct Tape. They'll fold up for storage and carrying as well as stand by themselves.

- Machine-stitching a piece of slippery material can be maddening. Put a piece of Reynolds Cut-Rite Wax Paper on the seam. Tear off when finished sewing.

- Before hand-painting T-shirts and other fabrics, cover the backing board with Reynolds Cut-Rite Wax Paper. It will keep the mess to a minimum.

- Display dried leaves or pressed flowers by affixing them to Reynolds Parchment Paper with Elmer's Glue-All. Add a colorful mat; frame.

PET-POURRI

- When training new puppies or cats, try this trick to keep them off the furniture: Place pieces of Reynolds Wrap Aluminum Foil on the seats. The new pets won't like the rustling sound and will learn to stay away.

- To deter cats from jumping on a sofa, wrap the pillows in Reynolds Wrap Aluminum Foil.

- If, however, you scrunch up a piece of Reynolds Wrap Aluminum Foil into a ball, your cat will thank you for the new toy!

- Clean pet hair off furniture or clothes with a sheet of GLAD Press'n Seal.

- Keep your kitty's nose out of your beverage by putting a circle of GLAD Press'n Seal on the top of your glass.

- For quicker cleanup, line the bottom of a litter box with GLAD Press'n Seal.

OUTDOOR LIVING

- Buzzing bees keeping you from drinking your beverage? Cover the top of the glass with a small square of Reynolds Wrap Aluminum Foil. Poke a drinking straw through it, and enjoy.

- For a disposable platter to take to picnics or other outings, cover a piece of cardboard with Reynolds Wrap Heavy Strength Aluminum Foil.

- Wrap a bit of Reynolds Wrap Aluminum Foil around a fishing hook. Fringe the foil, and the wiggling action just might lure a fish.

- Attention soccer moms and dads and everyone else: Bring a roll of GLAD Press'n Seal to cover a bench so you can stay dirt-free while watching a game or match.

- Is the wind threatening to blow away your picnic tablecloth? Secure it with Scotch Duct Tape under the table.

- Patch holes in children's pools—whether molded plastic or vinyl blow-up style—with Scotch Duct Tape. (Drain and dry the pool first.)

- Help soften the stiff leather of a new baseball mitt by adding Vaseline Petroleum Jelly to the palm. Rub in thoroughly and shape the glove around a ball. Secure with rubber bands overnight.

Glue Trap for Bugs

If nearly invisible bugs such as mites have attacked your plants, try this:

　8 ounces Elmer's Glue-All
　2 gallons warm water

Thoroughly mix the ingredients in a bucket. Pour the solution into a labeled spray bottle, and spray all twigs and leaves of your sad plants. The insects will be caught and will flake off with the sticky mess when it dries.

- To strengthen the wrist that powers your golf swing, open and close an extra-large binder clip.

GETAWAYS MADE GOOD

Travel Tips

- You're checking into a hotel or motel late at night, the kitchen is closed (or nonexistent), and items from a vending machine or overpriced minibar won't cut it. The problem is solved if you've packed some cheese sandwiches wrapped in Reynolds Wrap Aluminum Foil. Use the innkeeper's iron to press both sides of the wrapped snacks, and hot nutrition is yours in the form of freshly grilled cheese sandwiches.

- Protect your shoes from scuffs and your clothes from dirt: Wrap the shoes in GLAD Press'n Seal before packing them in your suitcase.

- Use two small pieces of GLAD Press'n Seal to carry vitamins or other pills.

- Put bright-colored strips of Scotch Duct Tape on your luggage. You'll ID your bags from a distance at the baggage claim. (Duct tape does double duty on luggage repair as well, if necessary.)

- The sticky-backed portion of a Post-it Note makes a great temporary label for travel bottles and jars.

- Write driving directions on a large Post-it Note. Stick it where you can see it easily and safely, such as on the dashboard or in the middle of the steering wheel.

Camping

◆ To clean dirty pots and pans while on a camping trip, scrunch up Reynolds Wrap Aluminum Foil into a ball and use as a pot scrubber. (Don't do this on Teflon-coated pans!)

◆ Make a lantern shine even brighter with Reynolds Wrap Aluminum Foil. Wrap a piece of wood or cardboard in foil, shiny side out, and place behind the light.

◆ A long sheet of Reynolds Wrap Heavy Strength Aluminum Foil under your sleeping bag provides protection from moisture.

◆ Keep your feet warm during cold-weather camping: Wrap some stones in Reynolds Wrap Aluminum Foil and heat them by the campfire. Transfer the hot stones to a towel; wrap and place at the foot of your sleeping bag.

◆ Keep matches dry in the great, but often damp, out-doors. Wrap them in Reynolds Wrap Aluminum Foil.

◆ Use Scotch Duct Tape to repair your tent, backpack, rubber boots, kayak, rain slicker, or nearly anything else that needs fixing.

◆ Store condiments for camp cooking (salt, pepper, spices, and more) in drinking straws. Fold over the end of a straw, and secure it closed with a small rubber band. Pour a spice into the straw, then fold over and secure the other end with another rubber band. Label the straw with a marking pen.

Trademark Information

Argo Corn Starch® is a registered trademark of the ACH Food Companies, Inc.

ARM & HAMMER® is a registered trademark of Church & Dwight Co., Inc.

Brillo Steel Wool Soap Pad® is a registered trademark of Church & Dwight Co., Inc.

Crayola® is a registered trademark of Binney & Smith Properties, Inc.

Crest® is a registered trademark of Procter & Gamble.

Elmer's® is a registered trademark of Borden.

GLAD® is a registered trademark of Union Carbide Corporation.

Gold Medal® is a registered trademark of General Mills, Inc.

Griffin® is a registered trademark of Hickory Brands, Inc.

Krazy® is a registered trademark of Borden.

McCormick® is a registered trademark of McCormick & Company, Incorporated.

Melitta Basket Coffee Filter® is a registered trademark of the Melitta Group.

O-Cel-O® is a registered trademark of 3M.

Pepsi® is a registered trademark of PepsiCo, Inc.

Post-it® is a registered trademark of 3M.

Q-tips® is a registered trademark of Chesebrough-Pond's USA Co.

Reynolds Wrap® is a registered trademark of Reynolds Metals.

Scotch® is a registered trademark of 3M.

Scott Towels® is a registered trademark of Kimberly-Clark Worldwide, Inc.

Vaseline® is a registered trademark of Chesebrough-Pond's USA Co.